What Makes a Plant?

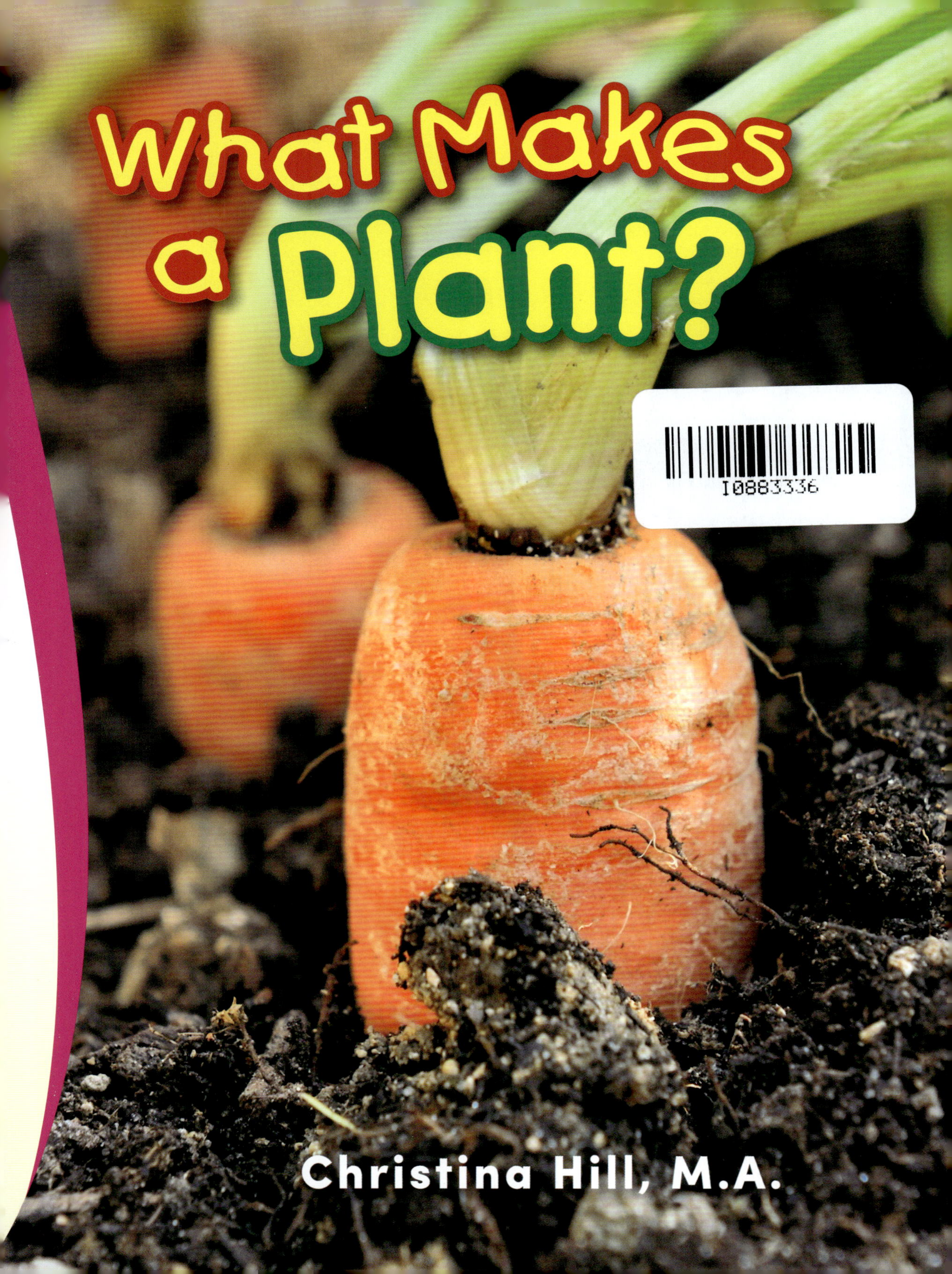

I0883336

Christina Hill, M.A.

Consultants

Sally Creel, Ed.D.
Curriculum Consultant

Leann Iacuone, M.A.T., NBCT, ATC
Riverside Unified School District

Jill Tobin
California Teacher of the Year
Semi-Finalist
Burbank Unified School District

Image Credits: pp.3, 8–9 iStock; p.4 Rick Goldwasser Photography/Flickr (CC-BY); pp.20–21 (illustrations) Chris Sabatino; all other images from Shutterstock.

Library of Congress Cataloging-in-Publication Data

Hill, Christina, author.
What makes a plant? / Christina Hill; consultants, Sally Creel, Ed.D. curriculum consultant, Leann Iacuone, M.A.T., NBCT, ATC, Riverside Unified School District, Jill Tobin, California Teacher of the Year Semi-Finalist, Burbank Unified School District.
pages cm
Summary: "Plants are living things. They go through a life cycle. Learn more about what plants need to live and grow"— Provided by publisher.
Audience: K to grade 3.
Includes index.
ISBN 978-1-4807-4559-9 (pbk.)
ISBN 978-1-4807-5049-4 (ebook)
1. Plants—Juvenile literature.
2. Plant life cycles—Juvenile literature. I. Title.
QK731.H516 2015
580—dc23

2014013138

Teacher Created Materials
5301 Oceanus Drive
Huntington Beach, CA 92649-1030
http://www.tcmpub.com

ISBN 978-1-4807-4559-9

© 2015 Teacher Created Materials, Inc.

Table of Contents

Life Cycle

Plants are living things that grow and change over time.

Grandpa Tree

The oldest tree is over 4,000 years old!

They have **life cycles** (SAHY-kuhlz).

A plant starts its life cycle as a seed.

The seed needs water, air, soil, and sunlight.

First, the seed grows **roots** in the soil, or dirt.

The roots help the plant **absorb** (ab-SAWRB) water.

This tree has large roots which help it get water.

Next, the **stem** grows.

This plant grows roots and then a stem.

It carries water and food through the plant.

Big Stems

A tree trunk is just a huge stem!

The plant also grows **leaves**. The leaves absorb sunlight.

Lots of Leaves

There are many different kinds of leaves. They come in lots of shapes and sizes.

Sunlight helps the plant make food.

Some plants grow **flowers**.

This is a yellow dandelion flower.

The flowers make seeds that grow into new plants.

This girl blows dandelion seeds.

New Plants

The new plant will look like its parent plant.

A new plant grows from a corn seed.

The new plant will grow leaves and seeds, too.

New seeds grow inside these tomatoes.

seeds

The life cycle begins again!

Let's Do Science!

What are the parts of a plant? Try this and see!

What to Get

- paper and pencil
- plant (with roots)
- scissors

What to Do

1. Look closely at your plant. What are the different parts?

2. Carefully cut apart your plant. Sort the parts.

3. Make a chart like this one. Place the parts of the plant on your chart.

leaves	
stems	
roots	
flowers	

4. Tell someone how you sorted the plant parts. Talk about what you think each part does.

Glossary

absorb—to take in or drink

flowers—the parts of the plant that make seeds

leaves—the flat parts of a plant that grow from the stem

life cycles—series of stages that living things go through as they grow older

roots—the parts of a plant that grow underground and absorb water

stem—the part of a plant that holds up the leaves and flowers

Index

Your Turn!

Tasty Plants

We eat many parts of plants. Peas are seeds. Carrots are roots. Lettuce is a leaf. Broccoli is a flower. Make a list of your favorite plants to eat. What part of the plant do they come from?